W9-BUF-717

Thinking Critically: LGBT Issues

Other titles in the *Thinking Critically* series include:

Thinking Critically
Thinking Critically: LGBT Issues

Don Nardo

ReferencePoint
Press®

San Diego, CA

© 2020 ReferencePoint Press, Inc.
Printed in the United States

For more information, contact:
ReferencePoint Press, Inc.
PO Box 27779
San Diego, CA 92198
www.ReferencePointPress.com

Picture Credits:
10: Rawpixel.com/Shutterstock.com
Charts and graphs by Maury Aaseng

LIBRARY OF CONGRESS CATALOGING-IN-PUBLICATION DATA

Names: Nardo, Don, 1947– author.
Title: Thinking Critically: LGBT Issues/by Don Nardo.
Description: San Diego, CA: ReferencePoint Press, Inc., [2020] | Series: Thinking Critically |
    Audience: Grade 9 to 12.
Identifiers: LCCN 2019002665 (print) | LCCN 2019017745 (ebook) | ISBN 9781682826621 (eBook)
    | ISBN 9781682826614 (hardback)
Subjects: LCSH: Sexual minorities—Juvenile literature. | Sexual minorities—Legal status, laws,
    etc.—Juvenile literature. | Sexual minorities—Civil rights—Juvenile literature.
Classification: LCC HQ73 (ebook) | LCC HQ73 .N37 2020 (print) | DDC 306.76—dc23
LC record available at https://lccn.loc.gov/2019002665

Contents

Foreword

"Literacy is the most basic currency of the knowledge economy we're living in today." Barack Obama (at the time a senator from Illinois) spoke these words during a 2005 speech before the American Library Association. One question raised by this statement is: What does it mean to be a literate person in the twenty-first century?

E.D. Hirsch Jr., author of *Cultural Literacy: What Every American Needs to Know*, answers the question this way: "To be culturally literate is to possess the basic information needed to thrive in the modern world. The breadth of the information is great, extending over the major domains of human activity from sports to science."

But literacy in the twenty-first century goes beyond the accumulation of knowledge gained through study and experience and expanded over time. Now more than ever literacy requires the ability to sift through and evaluate vast amounts of information and, as the authors of the Common Core State Standards state, to "demonstrate the cogent reasoning and use of evidence that is essential to both private deliberation and responsible citizenship in a democratic republic."

The *Thinking Critically* series challenges students to become discerning readers, to think independently, and to engage and develop their skills as critical thinkers. Through a narrative-driven, pro/con format, the series introduces students to the complex issues that dominate public discourse—topics such as gun control and violence, social networking, and medical marijuana. Each chapter revolves around a single, pointed question such as Can Stronger Gun Control Measures Prevent Mass Shootings?, or Does Social Networking Benefit Society?, or Should Medical Marijuana Be Legalized? This inquiry-based approach introduces student researchers to core issues and concerns on a given topic. Each chapter includes one part that argues the affirmative and one part that argues the negative—all written by a single author. With the single-author format the predominant arguments for and against an issue can be synthesized into clear, accessible discussions supported by details and evidence including relevant facts, direct quotes, current examples, and statistical illustrations. All volumes include focus questions to guide students as they read each pro/con discussion, a list of key facts, and an annotated list of related organizations and websites for conducting further research.

The authors of the Common Core State Standards have set out the particular qualities that a literate person in the twenty-first century must have. These include the ability to think independently, establish a base of knowledge across a wide range of subjects, engage in open-minded but discerning reading and listening, know how to use and evaluate evidence, and appreciate and understand diverse perspectives. The new *Thinking Critically* series supports these goals by providing a solid introduction to the study of pro/con issues.

LGBT Issues

American public attitudes toward LGBT people and their civil rights have changed dramatically over the past fifty years or so. (The acronym *LGBT* stands for lesbian, gay, bisexual, and transgender.) Sociologist Tina Fetner briefly sums up what it was like for members of that group of Americans as recently as 1955, saying, "Police routinely raided lesbian and gay bars, arresting patrons and publishing their names and addresses in the paper. Sex between two women or two men was illegal, and homosexuality was understood by psychiatrists to be a mental illness. In many places it was illegal for women to dance with women, or men with men."[1]

As a result of these negative societal attitudes and rules, most gay people chose to remain "in the closet," or to keep their sexual orientation hidden from others. Those who stepped out of the closet, or were outed by others, often faced name-calling, overt discrimination, rejection by family and friends, and/or loss of their jobs. Some even suffered physical attacks, a phenomenon that came to labeled *gay bashing*.

A Rapid Shift in Public Opinion

In marked contrast, by 2018 twenty-one US states had passed laws prohibiting discrimination on the basis of sexual orientation, and eighteen of those states had also banned discrimination against transgender people. It was, moreover, unlawful in many American cities and counties to discriminate against gay and lesbian people. In addition, rules against such discrimination were in place among federal employees and contractors. What is more, the US Equal Employment Opportunity Commission advocated that lesbian and gay people should benefit from federal antidiscrimination laws in their workplaces.

Perhaps the most astounding change in public attitudes and laws surrounding LGBT issues has been the acceptance and legalization of same-sex marriage. During the mid- to late twentieth century, most Americans said they found it unacceptable. Indeed, when the well-known public polling organization Gallup first asked Americans to give their opinions about same-sex marriage in 1996, only 27 percent responded that they supported it. Yet in what has been seen by many as an amazingly rapid shift in public opinion, a mere two decades later, in 2018, Gallup found that 67 percent, or two-thirds, of Americans had come to accept and even approve of same-sex marriage.

This swift and decisive change in public attitudes was also clearly reflected in the legal system's response to that controversial issue. In 2004 Massachusetts became the first US state to legalize same-sex marriage; Connecticut followed suit in 2008, as did Vermont in 2009. In the five years that followed, several other states did the same. In the wake of these fast-falling barriers, on June 26, 2015, the Supreme Court ruled that the US Constitution guarantees everyone, including same-sex couples, the right to marry. Announcing the court's majority opinion, Associate Justice Anthony Kennedy said, "The Court, in this decision, holds same-sex couples may exercise the fundamental right to marry in all States."[2]

Perhaps not surprisingly, the national legalization of same-sex marriage—a development that many LGBT people had assumed they would never live to see—inspired a flurry of weddings across the nation. Large numbers of lesbian, gay, bisexual, and transgender people took full advantage of the situation. In 2017, just two years after the high court's landmark decision, more than 10 percent of LGBT adults were legally married to a same-sex spouse.

Progress: A Long, Hard Process

This progress had occurred only because numerous members of the LGBT community, along with a fair number of their supporters, had worked long and hard to replace discrimination with equality and justice. As Fetner puts it, "In a country that has been reticent to guarantee equal rights to lesbian and gay people, this marks an important step forward in the slow, hard-fought battle for full citizenship."[3]

LGBT activists initiated that battle during the mid- to late twentieth century by organizing their community. Across the country, LGBT people steadily moved to LGBT-friendly neighborhoods in cities. These were seen as relatively safe spaces in which to live one's life without fear of blatant discrimination and hatred. In time those neighborhoods became hubs of LGBT culture and, as Fetner says, communities that strengthened collective identities.

Same-sex marriage now has widespread support among Americans. As of 2018, polls showed that two-thirds of Americans had come to accept and even approve of same-sex marriage.

As a result, the LGBT community became increasingly less fearful and more open. "Annual pride parades spread across the country into big cities and small towns alike, making LGBT lives visible to wider audiences," Fetner continues. "Lesbian and gay lives began to appear on television shows, in movies, and in the news." These trends helped improve the formerly negative image of LGBT people. In that more enlightened atmosphere, she says, "more and more cities and states began to make it illegal to discriminate on the basis of sexual orientation and gender identity."[4]

Attempts to Reverse Gains?

Yet, many LGBT activists point out, despite that progress and society's current widespread acceptance of LGBT people, the battle for their civil rights has not been won conclusively. Vocal segments of American society still do not support special protections for LGBT individuals. "Gays don't want equal rights, they want special rights," says one individual. "And if you don't agree with [their] lifestyle for whatever reason, you're a homophobe! Give me a break!"[5] Even as late as 2018, such attitudes appeared to threaten a number of gains that the LGBT community had made over the course of more than half a century.

Some activists, legal experts, and others close to the ongoing fight for LGBT rights place a large portion of the blame for this development on President Donald Trump and leaders within his administration. Others believe that Trump and his associates are only a symptom of a larger malady that the LGBT community has yet to overcome. In this view, Trump is merely a strong public voice for various religious, social, and political groups who think that LGBT people are undeserving of full civil rights protections.

Putting aside who is to blame for ongoing threats to recent LGBT civil rights gains, gay writer and editor Gabriel Arana says that those threats are very real. "Legal rights for gays and lesbians, for the most part, stood firm in the first year of Trump's presidency," he states. Nevertheless, he adds,

the administration has launched a full-scale attack on transgender people, who are most at risk because their rights are not as legally secure as gay rights. The administration is packing the federal judiciary with anti-LGBT appointees as quickly as possible, and the decisions those judges make now could harm the trans community for decades.[6]

More specifically, says Dan Diamond, a reporter for the Virginia-based journalism and news organization Politico, the Trump administration made several overt attempts to reverse gains that transgender folk had made during the preceding administration of President Barack Obama. Perhaps most notably, Trump tried to keep trans people from serving in the military. They had achieved that right in June 2016, during Obama's last year as president. A federal court temporarily stopped Trump's attempt to keep trans people out of the armed services, but in January 2019 the US Supreme Court ruled that the ban could go into effect.

> "The Trump administration has stopped even counting the number of LGBT citizens in the country. In effect, this makes [those citizens] invisible to lawmakers who are drafting legislation."[8]
>
> —Gay writer and editor Gabriel Arana

In addition, LGBT activists maintain, Trump's first attorney general (head of the US Department of Justice), Jeff Sessions, initiated another attempt to stifle transgender rights. The issue of which public bathrooms trans people should use had become controversial in 2015 and 2016. The anti-trans view was that they should use only the bathrooms labeled with their birth gender; the pro-trans view was that they should be allowed to use the ones labeled with the gender with which they identify. The Obama administration had issued a directive siding with the pro-trans view. But Trump reversed that directive. Moreover, according to Diamond, in February 2018 the US Department of Education "said that it would no longer investigate transgender students' complaints about access to bathrooms."[7]

Loud to Be Proud

Activists and others also say that the government has made it more difficult to ascertain how many LGBT people are in the country. Arana explains why this is important, saying,

> Part of the way government allocates resources to its citizens is by knowing who its people are. But the Trump administration has stopped even counting the number of LGBT citizens in the country. In effect, this makes [those citizens] invisible to lawmakers who are drafting legislation. . . . [For] the government to fail to keep [these] statistics [is] to rob us of our right to advocate for ourselves. [It is] one of the small things Trump has done that will have major consequences later.[8]

Thus, although the LGBT community benefited from many gains during the past several decades, its members have not attained a secure legal and social footing. As a result, activists warn, LGBT people and their friends and supporters need to keep demanding and working to solidify their civil rights. Arana, who is one such activist, says that to stop those rights from eroding any further, LGBT people "have to do something they're good at: being vocal so the public remembers we're under attack." He concludes, "Remember: before you can be proud, you have to be loud!"[9]

Chapter One

Should Same-Sex Marriage Be Allowed?

Same-Sex Marriage Should Not Be Allowed

- Marriage has always been, and should continue to be, strictly between one man and one woman.
- Marriage is for procreation of the species, and LGBT couples cannot procreate.
- The federal government does not have the authority to determine for the individual states whether to allow same-sex marriage.

The Debate at a Glance

Same-Sex Marriage Should Be Allowed

- Denying same-sex couples the right to marry violates their constitutional rights.
- Marriage is not simply for procreation.
- Marriage is about love and commitment between two people, regardless of their genders.

Same-Sex Marriage Should Not Be Allowed

"Same-sex marriage would only further undercut the procreative norm long associated with marriage insofar as it establishes that there is no necessary link between procreation and marriage."

—Family Research Council, a conservative Christian public policy group

Family Research Council, "Ten Arguments from Social Science Against Same-Sex Marriage," 2019. www.frc.org.

Consider these questions as you read:

1. Do you believe the laws of nature are merely descriptions of the way the world is, or are they principles that govern how the world works? Explain your answer.
2. Do you believe that the central role of marriage is, or should be, procreation? Why or why not?
3. Should states have the power to decide whether same-sex marriage is legal? Why or why not?

Editor's note: The discussion that follows presents common arguments made in support of this perspective, reinforced by facts, quotes, and examples taken from various sources.

A certain amount of order exists within the natural world. "The tides rise and fall, the moon has four phases . . . water slakes thirst, and persons grow older, not younger,"[10] states the Internet Encyclopedia of Philosophy. These are just a few of the laws of nature; they are constant and eternal. In a very real sense, the natural world obeys these laws.

The concept of marriage between a man and a woman can be viewed in this way as well. For, as everyone knows, marriage has always been an arrangement that builds on the natural pairing of male and female. "As we now understand it, marriage is not merely the expression of a love people have for each other," states essayist Michael Jensen, who is also the rector of St. Mark's Anglican Church in Darling Point, Australia. Marriage, he argues, "is intended as a life-long union between two people who exemplify the biological duality of the human race, with the openness to welcoming children into the world." A more concise way of saying this, he adds, is that "the institution of marriage has traditionally been defined as being between a man and a woman."[11]

Put simply, same-sex marriage defies the natural order. Those who support the idea of same-sex marriage pretend that the notion of two separate genders coming together as one through marriage is an arrangement crafted by humans—perhaps out of necessity. In presenting marriage this way, they ignore the fundamental rules of God and nature—that is, the natural pairing of man and woman.

> "It is through children alone that sexual relations become important to society."[13]
>
> —Noted philosopher Bertrand Russell

Advocates of same-sex marriage invariably object to characterizing marriage between a man and a woman as the natural—and therefore the superior—approach to marital unions. This is perhaps understandable. No one enjoys being labeled as unnatural, after all. Unfortunately, their all-too-common reaction is to brand advocates of traditional male-female marriage as biased. This is grossly unfair; but more importantly, it negates the legitimacy of such views. As Jensen states, "Having put that opinion forward, I fully recognize that there are many people of intelligence and good will who disagree. I do not expect to convince everyone. What I do hope is that my contribution [to this argument] will not be derided as bigoted or homophobic out of hand, but that it will be seen as part of a civil discussion."[12]

The Human Urge to Reproduce

Another potent argument against same-sex marriage is that the principal purpose of that venerable institution is procreation: having children and

Many Americans Still Oppose Same-Sex Marriage

Despite the fact that opposition to same-sex marriage has fallen among conservatives since the Supreme Court legalized it in 2015, a large number of conservative, religiously devout Americans still think it should not be allowed.

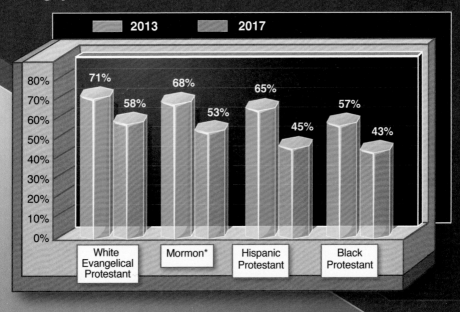

Percentage of each group that was opposed to allowing gay and lesbian couples to marry legally in . . .

2013   2017

White Evangelical Protestant: 71% (2013), 58% (2017)
Mormon*: 68% (2013), 53% (2017)
Hispanic Protestant: 65% (2013), 45% (2017)
Black Protestant: 57% (2013), 43% (2017)

* The 2013 Mormon figure is based on research conducted in 2014.

Source: PRRI/Brookings 2013 Religion, Values & Immigration Reform Survey; PRRI 2014 American Values Atlas; PRRI 2017 American Values Atlas. Reprinted in "Emerging Consensus on LGBT Issues," 2017. www.prri.org.

thereby perpetuating the human species. The great Nobel Prize–winning philosopher Bertrand Russell wrote in 1929, "It is through children alone that sexual relations become important to society, and worthy to be taken cognizance of [recognized] by a legal institution."[13]

Echoing that same thought was a July 2014 legal brief filed by attorneys defending the same-sex marriage ban then in effect in Arizona. It argued, "The State regulates marriage for the primary purpose of channeling potentially procreative sexual relationships into enduring unions for the sake of joining children to both their mother and their father. [But] same-sex couples can never provide a child with both her biological mother and her biological father."[14]

It is true that gay and lesbian people can adopt a child, which is legal in all fifty states. But because same-sex couples cannot produce their own biological offspring, they should not be granted the privilege of getting married. Therefore, the US Supreme Court's 2015 ruling that made same-sex marriage legal in all fifty states was a serious error.

No one is stopping gay and lesbian people from living together as roommates or close friends or even in civil unions. Furthermore, if they have a strong desire to raise children, adoption is a viable option. Admittedly, there are heterosexual couples who say they do not wish to have children. In such cases, however, the potential still exists for them to have children at some future date if they change their minds.

Indeed, the importance of the human urge and need to procreate cannot be overstressed. One argument often heard in support of same-sex marriage is that even if the couple cannot have children, they have a right to enjoy a sexual relationship within the bounds of marriage. No doubt they do have a right to have a sexual relationship, and no one is suggesting that they be denied that. But sexual relations between a man and woman are different from—and superior to—same-sex sexual relations for the very reason that the potential for new life exists when a male and female mate. The human race could not continue to replicate itself without that biological dynamic, from which gay and lesbian relationships are excluded.

Let the States Decide

Ignoring the laws of nature, the Supreme Court chose to make same-sex marriage legal nationwide in 2015. Not only does this decision defy the laws of nature; it also usurps the right of individual states to make that determination. The concept of states' rights is well established in US law. From the country's earliest years, its leaders were careful not to give the federal government so much power that it would overpower the rights of individual states to decide their own destinies. A balance between federal authority and states' rights was then, and remains, the foundation of the political concept of federalism.

One important aspect of federalism is that the federal government should not be in the business of telling people how to live their lives. If the residents of a state have the right to determine things such as town boundaries and property taxes, they should also be able to decide whether or not to accept same-sex marriage. Seventy-five-year-old retired Arizona teacher Frances Narramore speaks for many people when she says, "The federal government is too involved in too many personal things that they don't need to be involved in."[15]

That same attitude was reflected prominently in a *New York Times*/CBS News poll taken in 2013, just two years before the Supreme Court made its highly divisive ruling on same-sex marriage. Queried as to whether same-sex marriage rights should be determined by the federal government or left to each individual state government to decide, fully 60 percent of the respondents said they preferred having the states make that decision. Only 33 percent felt that the federal government should be involved.

> "Leaving this issue [of same-sex marriage] to the democratic processes of the states preserves a foundational element of freedom."[17]
>
> —Legal scholars Eric Restuccia and Aaron Lindstrom

Not surprisingly, these percentages were roughly matched by the attitudes of the national legislators representing those who responded to the survey. In early 2015, many Republican legislators called on the Supreme Court to refrain from reviewing the issue of same-sex marriage or to uphold the prohibition on same-sex marriage that existed at the time in several states. As *U.S. News & World Report* writer Kenneth T. Walsh explains, "Much of the GOP [Republican] argument rests on the concept of letting the states work out their own solutions rather than imposing a one-size-fits-all approach from on high. On the other side of the issue, many gay-marriage supporters filed briefs arguing that fairness demands allowing same-sex marriage as a national policy."[16]

Of course, as history subsequently showed, the nine justices ignored the pleas to maintain the status quo on the contentious issue of same-sex marriage. They legalized it for the nation as a whole. That decision, many thoughtful people believe, represents a serious blow to the idea of a balance between the powers of the states and the federal government. For more than two centuries, some issues have traditionally been left to the states to wrestle with; other issues have been better decided by the federal government. Issues concerning marriage are "a matter for the states," legal scholars Eric Restuccia and Aaron Lindstrom rightly contend. "Ultimately, leaving this issue to the democratic processes of the states preserves a foundational element of freedom: the right of the people to govern themselves. The power to define marriage is theirs alone."[17]

The legalization of same-sex marriage on a nationwide scale was a mistake. It defies the laws of nature and ignores the well-established principle of states' rights.

Same-Sex Marriage Should Be Allowed

"I fall in love with a person and not a gender."

—Bisexual Swiss college student Runa Wehrl

Quoted in Katy Romy, "'I Fall in Love with a Person and Not a Gender,'" Swissinfo, October 9, 2017. www.swissinfo.ch.

Consider these questions as you read:

1. Do you believe that history should be a guide when considering whether same-sex marriage should be allowed? Explain your answer.
2. What are some of the reasons why couples no longer see having children as the primary purpose for marriage? What is your view of the purpose of marriage?
3. What do you think would be the effect of a reversal by the Supreme Court of its 2015 decision legalizing same-sex marriage? Explain.

Editor's note: The discussion that follows presents common arguments made in support of this perspective, reinforced by facts, quotes, and examples taken from various sources.

Marriage is not a privilege to be granted or not granted by the government. Whether to marry—and whom to marry—is an individual choice. Same-sex couples have as much right as heterosexual couples to make these determinations and to have their unions be fully recognized under the law. A majority of the members of the US Supreme Court recognized this when they legalized same-sex marriage in 2015. Yet a number of individuals and groups are searching for ways to challenge and reverse that landmark decision.

Such opponents of same-sex marriage frequently point out that marriage, throughout time and in cultures around the globe, has traditionally been an arrangement between a man and a woman. But history, as has been seen on many occasions, should not always be a guide. The fact that ancient Romans and colonial Americans, among others, disdained the practice of same-sex marriage does not mean that people today should do so. After all, nearly all past societies accepted and practiced slavery. Most also treated women as men's political and moral inferiors. Just as those antiquated societal attitudes and practices were eventually proved morally wrong and were eliminated, so, too, has been the ban on same-sex marriage.

The US founders, who crafted the Constitution, did not at that time foresee that same-sex marriage would ever be a serious topic of discussion. Therefore, they did not address that issue in creating the structural and legal blueprint for the new nation. Nevertheless, same-sex marriage can be seen as falling within a broad principle the founders articulated in writing the Constitution. That principle is known as equal protection of the laws. It means that the nation's laws apply to and protect each citizen, who is considered equal to all other citizens.

> "[Marriage] law was not written to require that we live forever with the limited perspectives of past generations."[18]
>
> —Political scientist Robert de Neufville

It is not important that same-sex marriage is not specifically mentioned in the Constitution. Many events of modern life—such as the right to privacy and the right to vote—do not appear anywhere in that noble document, yet the courts have determined that the Constitution protects people's right to privacy and to vote. That is the beauty of the Constitution; it was written to serve as the guiding principles for life in America for all time. "To read the laws as nothing more than the narrow intentions of their authors is to ignore what the laws actually say," explains political scientist Robert de Neufville. He continues,

> By writing that no state "shall deprive any person of life, liberty, or property, without due process of law; nor deny to any person within its jurisdiction the equal protection of the laws" the authors of the [Constitution] required each generation to use its best judgment about what life, liberty, and property mean, and

Public support for same-sex marriage grew rapidly between 1996 and 2018. In a 2018 Gallup poll, 67 percent said that marriages between same-sex couples should be recognized by law as valid and that those couples should enjoy the same rights as traditional male-female couples.

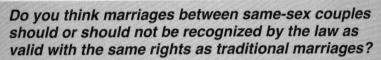

Do you think marriages between same-sex couples should or should not be recognized by the law as valid with the same rights as traditional marriages?

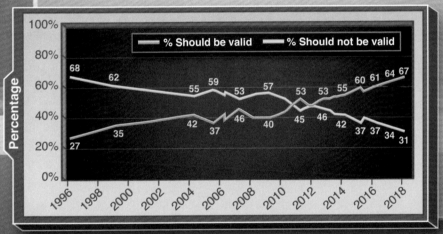

Source: Justin McCarthy, at Gallup, "Two in Three Americans Support Same-Sex Marriage," May 2018. https://news.gallup.com.

about what the equal protection of the laws entails. The law was not written to require that we live forever with the limited perspectives of past generations, but rather that we interpret it by our own [situation] as well as we can.[18]

Thus, equal protection is not for a privileged few but rather for everyone. That means that everyone has the right to marry whomever they please. "This is the very essence of the idea of human rights," Neufville argues. "Not everyone will choose to marry or even welcome the opportunity. But everyone should have the choice."[19]

The Biological Factor

Although marriage was once strictly viewed as an arrangement for having children, this thinking has changed dramatically over time. Many couples still view marriage this way, but many do not. A 2018 Pew Research Center poll found that having children is a distant fourth on the list of reasons why people get married today, well behind love, making a lifelong commitment, and companionship.

Thus, the idea that couples get married mainly to produce offspring is plainly untrue. Simple reasoning shows that procreation and marriage are often two separate issues in modern society. If marriage consisted principally of males and females uniting to have children, then all couples who planned *not* to have children would need to be denied the right to marry. Imagine the public outcry if a town, state, or Congress tried to pass such a law.

Moreover, there is the issue of heterosexual couples who find that they are biologically unable to conceive children. Should they, too, be barred from getting married? By the same reasoning, elderly people who are too old to produce children should also be banned from getting married. This very idea seems absurd. Yet for centuries gay and lesbian couples were told they could not marry because they could not procreate, but infertile and elderly couples without children had full marriage rights.

These arguments might seem moot now, considering that the Supreme Court legalized same-sex marriage in 2015. Yet some sectors of society objected to that decision and would like to see the high court reverse itself on this matter. Consider what would happen if the court did that and cited as a reason the fact that gay and lesbian couples cannot procreate. To be fair and evenhanded, the same interpretation would need to be applied to heterosexual couples. As Austin Cline, director for the Council for Secular Humanism, describes it,

> Even if we didn't outlaw both contraception and abortion, we would have to take steps to ensure that all married couples are not childless: if they won't produce their own kids, they will have to adopt some of the many orphaned and abandoned children

currently without stable homes and families. Since we don't see anyone arguing for such outrageous measures, we must conclude that opponents of same-sex marriage don't take that principle as seriously as they seem.[20]

Society Is Strengthened, Not Weakened

Indeed, no such outrageous measures should ever be necessary because many of the Americans who opposed same-sex marriage in the past are steadily but surely coming to recognize what marriage is actually about. Put simply, marriage is about love and commitment between two people, no matter their gender or sexual orientation. Even a number of religious groups have come around to this view. In July 2005, for example, the United Church of Christ General Synod, a prominent Christian denomination in the United States, publicly stated its support for "equal marriage rights for couples regardless of gender."[21]

The fact that love is the basis for the strongest marriages, no matter which genders or sexual orientations are involved, is reinforced by examining the case of noted transgender activist JamieAnn Meyers. "My wife and I met one another as seventh graders in 1957,"[22] Meyers recalls. The two went steady for a while and then married in 1966. They long remained happy together, having two children and later three grandchildren.

Despite enjoying a loving, successful marriage, Meyers goes on, one unusual issue haunted the relationship:

> "Our love has not been diminished by my gender transition. It's the same love we have always had for one another."[23]
>
> —Transgender woman JamieAnn Meyers

Throughout my life, a ghost lurked in the furthest corners of my mind. This ghost was my true self, my identity that I could never reveal to anyone, not even to myself. I was paralyzed by fears that were I to reveal my true self, I would most certainly lose everything, including my very life. You see, I'm a transgender woman.

The man who would later become JamieAnn finally came out as female to his wife, but the love between them was so strong that the marriage survived and became even stronger than ever. "Now that I'm finally whole in body and spirit," Meyers continues,

> we've found new strength, individually and together. We've found new ways of expressing our love, new ways of walking through life as two women in a stronger and ongoing committed relationship. [Moreover] our love has not been diminished by my gender transition. It's the same love we have always had for one another.[23]

Meyers emphasizes that an unorthodox marriage like hers is not a threat to more traditional male-female marriages. Nor do same-sex marriages threaten society as a whole. This is because there is plenty of room for all sorts of marriages in a society that is actually strengthened, rather than weakened, by diversity and tolerance.

Chapter Two

Should Transgender People Be Allowed to Serve in the Military?

Transgender People Should Not Be Allowed to Serve in the Military

- Trans people serving openly will destroy unit cohesion.
- The cost of health care and gender transitions for trans people will bankrupt the military.
- Transgenderism is a mental illness, and the military should not admit mentally ill people.

The Debate at a Glance

Transgender People Should Be Allowed to Serve in the Military

- Trans people are physically and mentally fit to serve in the military.
- Health care costs for trans people are no greater than health care costs for anyone else.
- Banning trans people from the military is unconstitutional.

Transgender People Should Not Be Allowed to Serve in the Military

"Our military must be focused on decisive and overwhelming victory and cannot be burdened with the tremendous medical costs and disruption that transgender in the military would entail."

—President Donald Trump

Quoted in Jeremy Redmon, "President Trump: No Transgender People Allowed in the U.S. Military," *Atlanta Journal-Constitution,* July 26, 2017. www.ajc.com.

Consider these questions as you read:

1. In what ways might a transgender service member affect unit cohesion, if at all? Explain your answer.
2. Do you agree that cost should be a factor in whether transgender people are allowed to join the military? Why or why not?
3. How much emphasis should be placed on mental health when determining who should be allowed to serve? Explain your answer.

Editor's note: The discussion that follows presents common arguments made in support of this perspective, reinforced by facts, quotes, and examples taken from various sources.

In July 2017 President Donald Trump announced, through a series of tweets, that the US government would no longer permit transgender people to serve in the military. His statement came about a year after the Pentagon had lifted a former prohibition against transgender people serving. "After consultation with my Generals and military experts," the president tweeted, "please be advised that the United States Government will not accept or allow Transgender individuals to serve in any capacity in the U.S. Military. Our military must be focused on decisive and overwhelming victory and cannot be burdened with the tremendous medical costs and disruption that transgender in the military would entail."[24]

Soon afterward, White House press secretary Sarah Sanders clarified Trump's remarks for members of the press. She said the president had concluded that transgender military service "erodes military readiness and unit cohesion and made his decision based on that." She added, "It's obviously a very difficult decision, not a simple one, but the president thinks it's the best one for the military."[25]

Trump's decision to reverse the more lenient policy set in motion by his predecessor, President Barack Obama, got a huge boost in January 2019 when the US Supreme Court ruled that Trump's anti-transgender order could go into effect. Obama might have meant well when he ordered the military to begin allowing transgender people to serve openly, but this decision was not well thought out. Transgender people simply do not belong in the military. And this is not just Trump's view. A 2017 *Military Times* poll found that close to 53 percent of active-duty troops agreed with the president's stance on the matter.

One of the most important reasons for this view is concern about the effect on unit cohesion. Military personnel must have full trust in each other and in their leaders. They must develop a strong sense of camaraderie. They must believe that all members of their unit will act in the best interests of the group. There can be no special privileges or accommodations for individual unit members if they are to function as a strong, cohesive group. Retired US Army lieutenant colonel and author Ralph Peters explains why this is so important and why allowing transgender individuals to serve is bad policy. Says Peters,

That platoon is a killing machine. Period. Whatever enhances its ability to destroy our enemies is good. Whatever hampers that ability is bad. And the weapons in that platoon are not nearly so important as leadership and cohesion. . . . An infantry platoon at war lives in physical misery, filth, exhaustion, overstretched nerves, fear—and camaraderie. . . . There are no special privileges.

A Majority of US Soldiers Oppose Transgender Military Service

This graphic shows that a majority of the members of the US military are against allowing transgender people to serve, which supports Trump's anti-transgender stance on the issue.

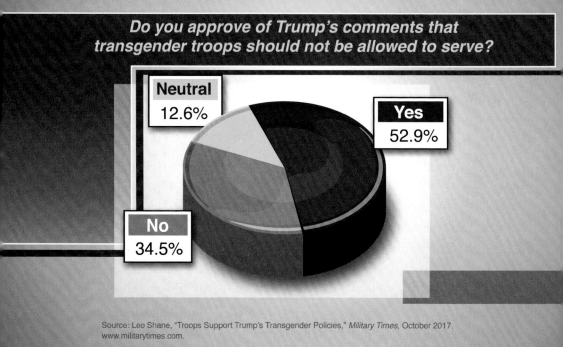

Do you approve of Trump's comments that transgender troops should not be allowed to serve?

Neutral
12.6%

Yes
52.9%

No
34.5%

Source: Leo Shane, "Troops Support Trump's Transgender Policies," *Military Times*, October 2017. www.militarytimes.com.

And there is no room for politically correct accommodations. . . . [Allowing] transgender personnel diverts attention from the platoon's primary purpose, killing the enemy.[26]

Much Too Costly

Another reason Trump gave for making his decision is that allowing transgender people to serve in the military will be far too costly for the country. Thomas Spoehr, the director of the Center for National Defense, explains, saying, "These individuals would need medical treatments—hormone therapies and, often, surgeries and the accompanying recovery times—throughout the duration of their service. On this basis alone, under existing rules applicable to all, they would not be allowed to join."[27]

The military routinely turns away people who have all sorts of health problems—including some that seem fairly insignificant, especially when contrasted with the major life change that transgender individuals undergo. This is a primary concern for Vicky Hartzler, a Republican congresswoman from Missouri. She explained her concern during a CNN interview:

> I had an intern who was denied the ability to go into the military because she had a bunion on her foot, and the argument was that this may cost the military and she might have to have surgery. Right now, we have people who cannot serve in the military with asthma or with flat feet. So why would we allow individuals to come in, although they're very patriotic and we appreciate their desire to serve, but who have medical problems that could be very costly? We shouldn't make an exception in this case.[28]

Hartzler went on to say that she had looked at the issue very closely. Transgender people have operations so that they can transform from one gender to the other, and the combination of the surgery and recovery is extremely costly. Her overall conclusion was that allowing transgender people to serve would cost US taxpayers $1.35 billion during the first ten years alone, mainly for sex reassignment surgeries. At least one other estimate, this one by the Family Research Council, places the cost at $3.7 billion. The military, which is funded by the taxpayers, would have to pick up that cost. Is this really how Americans want their tax dollars spent? And how would this

"Should we be spending any tax dollars to do gender reassignment surgeries when we have soldiers who don't have body armor or bullets?"[29]

—Vicky Hartzler, a Republican congresswoman from Missouri

affect the military's budget for other necessities? "Should we be spending any tax dollars to do gender reassignment surgeries when we have soldiers who don't have body armor or bullets?" Hartzler asks. "We need to be investing every dollar that we have to meet the threats that we're facing as a nation."[29]

Serious Emotional Difficulties

It is also important to note that many transgender people experience severe emotional distress, or gender dysphoria, as a result of their condition. This is a mental illness that requires a very specific type of care and treatment. No one is arguing that they should be disparaged for that disability. Nevertheless, someone who has serious mental or emotional difficulties should not be permitted to serve in the military.

Whether we like it or not—whether it is politically correct to say it or not—it is undeniable that someone who is experiencing a crisis involving gender identity will be under an enormous amount of stress. Does adding more extreme stress such as that which occurs in a war zone really make sense? "Are transgender individuals as mentally resilient and as able to withstand the extreme stresses of the harsh crucible of combat as non-transgender individuals?" asks Spoehr. Answering his own question, he reports that some studies have found that transgender people attempt suicide and feel psychologically distressed far more often than nontransgender people do. On the basis of that data, he states, "it would be both irresponsible and immoral to place such individuals in a position where they are exposed to the additional extraordinary stresses and pressures of the battlefield."[30]

Thus, although transgender people who want to serve should be commended for caring about their country, it would be better overall

> "It would be both irresponsible and immoral to place such individuals in a position where they are exposed to the additional extraordinary stresses and pressures of the battlefield."[30]
>
> —Thomas Spoehr, the director of the Center for National Defense

for the country if they do not serve. Unit cohesion will be adversely affected by their presence in the ranks, and military health care costs will skyrocket. Perhaps most important of all, transgender individuals who are experiencing severe emotional and personal inner turmoil should not be subjected to the extreme pressures of war. It is to some degree unfortunate and may seem unfair that someone who desires so much to serve cannot do so. But we must face a fact of life that affects all of us at one time or another—namely, that life is not always fair.

Transgender People Should Be Allowed to Serve in the Military

"Every day that goes by, [transgender] service members are doing a good job, showing the military and the world that they're fit, qualified, and capable."

—Shannon Minter, the legal director for the National Center for Lesbian Rights

Quoted in Samantha Allen, "Trump's Desperate Gamble on Asking SCOTUS to Rule on Transgender Troop Ban," Daily Beast, November 27, 2018. www.thedailybeast.com.

Consider these questions as you read:

1. If a transgender individual meets all military requirements, should he or she be accepted for military service? Why or why not?
2. Should medical treatment for transgender individuals be viewed differently than medical treatment for other military personnel? Why or why not?
3. In what sense does a ban on transgender individuals serving in the military violate the Constitution?

Editor's note: The discussion that follows presents common arguments made in support of this perspective, reinforced by facts, quotes, and examples taken from various sources.

"The Supreme Court just ended my military career. The justices chose not to protect the rights of transgender patriots like me," stated naval aviator and defense analyst Brynn Tannehill on January 22, 2019. Earlier that day the high court had ruled in a five-to-four decision that the Trump administration could reinstate its policy barring transgender people from serving in the military. "The decision," Tannehill continued, "was both a devastating blow to me personally, and a disturbing sign of what is to come for transgender people in the United States."[31]

Tannehill's misgivings are valid and justified. The often-repeated idea that transgender individuals are mentally or physically unfit for military service is absolute rubbish. Those who insist that transgender individuals are somehow less capable of serving in the military, or even serving with distinction in combat, do not know what they are talking about. Such comments are based on ignorance. Jay Caputo, a US Coast Guard officer who is both transgender and a widely recognized expert on transgender issues, points out that transgender individuals are simply ordinary people who identify with the opposite gender from the one they were assigned at birth.

The American Psychiatric Association does not classify transgenderism as a mental disorder. "In fact," says Caputo, "scientists have discovered that transgender brains more closely resemble the brains of the gender identified with than the gender assigned at birth. The body does not match the brain. Transgender individuals were born into the incorrect bodies."[32]

> **"Transgender individuals were born into the incorrect bodies."[32]**
>
> —US Coast Guard officer Jay Caputo

All that should matter is that the person who wishes to serve meets the standards used by the military for generations. What that means is that any person who wants to enlist and has a male body must meet male service standards; similarly, anyone with a female body must meet the female standards. As long as a trans person can meet those standards—and the vast majority of trans recruits *do* meet them—he or she should be considered physically fit to serve.

In fact, a number of high-placed military leaders have publicly stated their agreement with that idea. In part, that opinion is based on the fact that the proportion of active-duty transgender service people is tiny compared to the number of people who serve overall, which is in the millions. Although there is no official number, recent research estimates that there are up to about 10,790 transgender individuals on active duty or in reserve forces. Whatever their gender identity might be, such a small number of people scattered across the army, navy, and air force is hardly going to disrupt the military's enormous and well-disciplined ranks.

Only a Minority of Trans People Transition

Yet another objection that is frequently raised is that transgender service members will require transitioning treatment and surgery. This is usually framed around concerns about cost and disruption in function of military operations. This, Caputo explains, is "the most poorly understood aspect of whether transgender persons are fit to serve."[33] Not all trans military personnel choose to transition; in fact, only a small minority choose that option.

Those who *do* choose to transition are merely trying to correct a condition that they have had since birth. Many service members have surgery or treatment for a variety of conditions that, once corrected, do not impede their work. Says Caputo,

> Many types of physical "defects" can be corrected and meet military standards. A service member who is injured in combat, a car accident, or while playing sports on the weekend is provided medical treatment and allowed time to recover. Members who may temporarily be unfit for deployment because of injury, illness, medical condition, or mental health issues routinely are treated with medication, surgery, therapy, or other intervention and brought back to full fitness for duty. Having gender dysphoria is no different; it is correctable through treatment by transitioning.[34]

The Costs Are Relatively Low

Moreover, the cost of transitioning is not nearly as high as some have suggested. A study by the Rand Corporation, a widely respected nonprofit research organization that focuses on public policy, examined the costs of transition-related treatments for transgender service personnel and found them to be relatively low. In part, the study stated, this was because only a small number of transgender military personnel (between 29 and 129 people) actually sought treatment that could disrupt their ability to deploy. Furthermore, the individual costs of those operations ranged from $20,000 to $30,000. To put those costs in perspective, the

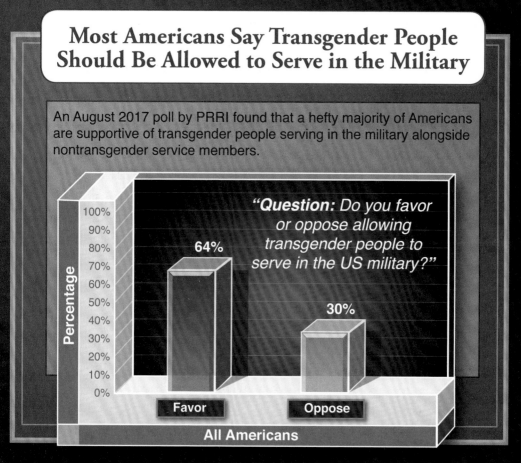

Most Americans Say Transgender People Should Be Allowed to Serve in the Military

An August 2017 poll by PRRI found that a hefty majority of Americans are supportive of transgender people serving in the military alongside nontransgender service members.

"Question: Do you favor or oppose allowing transgender people to serve in the US military?"

64%

30%

Favor

Oppose

All Americans

Percentage
100%
90%
80%
70%
60%
50%
40%
30%
20%
10%
0%

Source: PRRI, "Most Americans Oppose Restricting Rights for LGBT People," 2017. www.prri.org.

study found that, in comparison, far larger numbers of nontransgender military personnel had more costly surgeries to correct a variety of conditions. For instance, several thousand soldiers and sailors had knee replacements, which cost the taxpayers an average of $49,500 per knee.

Moreover, the study pointed out, the recovery time for knee surgery is seven to twelve weeks, during which the rehabilitating soldiers received their full pay. By contrast, the recovery time for even the most extensive transgender surgery was just six to eight weeks. Thus, the military pays much less for trans-related surgery and recovery than it does for standard knee operations and their recovery.

Knee surgeries constitute only one of many medical costs that the military pays for on a regular basis to keep its personnel both physically fit and psychologically content. Regarding the latter, the Pentagon's annual budget allows $41.6 million for Viagra and $22.8 million for Cialis. Both of these drugs have only one benefit: to enhance male sexual performance. In comparison, the same budget allots just $8.4 million in total for all transgender-related medical costs.

> "The court is aware of no argument or evidence suggesting that being transgender in any way limits one's ability to contribute to society."[36]
>
> —US district judge Colleen Kollar-Kotelly

That means that the US military—and, by extension, the government and taxpayers—spends almost $65 million a year on male sexual supplements. That is eight times more than is spent on the surgeries for trans personnel. Yet those who are against trans people serving claim a major reason for that position is that it is too expensive. Commenting on what is clearly a dishonest and foolish argument, award-winning educator Martie Sirois says that the $8.4 million spent on trans soldiers is "not a 'burden' on the military." Rather, "8.4 million pales in comparison to 65 million; I mean, let's be fiscally reasonable here."[35]

A Constitutional Question

That the costs of maintaining trans soldiers and sailors are relatively low is only one argument that was and continues to be leveled at Trump's ban on transgender military service. There is also the persuasive contention that such a prohibition is unconstitutional. Making that very point, in October 2017 US district judge Colleen Kollar-Kotelly blocked most of the ban Trump had issued the preceding July. She ruled that the policy violated the Constitution's guarantee of equal protection. Although her decision was overruled by the high court's January 2019 ruling, a different outcome could result the next time this issue reaches the Supreme Court.

In her ruling, Kollar-Kotelly noted that the government had failed to prove that transgender individuals represent a liability to the military ranks. "The court," she wrote, "is aware of no argument or evidence suggesting that being transgender in any way limits one's ability to contribute to society. The exemplary military service of plaintiffs in this case certainly suggests that it does not."[36]

In addition, the judge's groundbreaking ruling held that the government's reasons for banning trans troops are "not merely unsupported" and unconstitutional but are "actually contradicted by the studies, conclusions and judgments of the military itself." Citing the Rand study and other objective evidence, she concluded that "the needs of the military [are] best served by allowing transgender individuals to openly serve."[37] There is little doubt, therefore, that under the next president, trans people will again take their rightful place in the military ranks, where all brave and capable patriots who choose to serve belong.

Chapter Three

Are Employment Protections Needed for LGBT Workers?

Employment Protections Are Not Needed for LGBT Workers

- Protecting LGBT employees in the workplace violates the religious freedom of non-LGBT persons.
- Giving LGBT people such protections would grant them special protections that are not available to others.
- Giving such workplace protections is unnecessary because states, cities, and some businesses already have antidiscrimination policies in place.

The Debate at a Glance

Employment Protections Are Needed for LGBT Workers

- Granting LGBT people workplace protections does not violate anyone's religious freedom.
- Being able to work without being discriminated against or harassed is not a special privilege but rather a basic human right.
- Only a minority of states, cities, and companies have actually instituted antidiscrimination policies for LGBT people.

Employment Protections Are Not Needed for LGBT Workers

"The Federal Government should never be used as a tool to stamp out religious liberty—that principle which is so central to our Nation's founding and to human happiness itself."

—Mike Lee, US senator from Utah

Mike Lee, "Sen. Lee Objects to the Unanimous Consent of Chai Feldblum's Confirmation to the EEOC," Speech, December 19, 2018.

Consider these questions as you read:

1. Do you believe that earlier laws that outlaw discrimination based on sex should be interpreted to include sexual orientation and gender identity? Why or why not?
2. Why do some groups warrant special legal protection in the workplace but others do not—and is this fair? Explain your answer.
3. When it comes to discrimination in the workplace, can there ever be too many laws? Explain your answer.

Editor's note: The discussion that follows presents common arguments made in support of this perspective, reinforced by facts, quotes, and examples taken from various sources.

LGBT workers should not receive special employment protections simply because they are gay or transgender. Such workers should be subject to—and content with—the same workplace rules as non-LGBT workers. Unfortunately, LGBT rights groups are now trying to change those rules to suit their own needs. Sixteen states and the federal government find this to be unacceptable. The attorneys general of those states believe that business owners have the right to fire employees who behave in a way that violates the owner's religious views. In 2018 they asked the Supreme

Court to rule that an employer who takes this action for this reason is not violating federal workplace discrimination laws. The US Department of Justice (DOJ) filed a brief in support of this case a few months later.

Strongly Held Religious Beliefs

The crux of the argument by both the DOJ and the sixteen states is that earlier court rulings on behalf of transgender workers were based on a false premise. Those rulings were based on the view that Title VII of the Civil Rights Act of 1964 protects transgender workers. This is because Title VII says someone cannot be discriminated against because of his or her "sex." But as the states and the DOJ pointed out, the word *sex* in the 1964 act was a reference to one's biological sex—that is, being male or female. It had nothing to do with sexual orientation or gender identity.

This new interpretation of the law lies at the heart of the plight of a growing number of business owners who have religious objections to cross-dressing and other questionable displays by LGBT workers. Put simply, a business owner does not give up his or her constitutionally protected rights simply on account of owning that business. If the owner has a strongly held religious belief regarding LGBT issues, she or he should have the right to act on it without fear of legal retaliation.

This was the central issue in the case of Aimee Stephens, a Michigan funeral home director. In 2016 she informed her boss, Thomas Rost, that she planned to transition from male to female. Rost fired her, saying that he could not in good conscience allow her to dress as a woman at work. He argued that he was a devout Christian who believes "that the Bible teaches that God creates people male or female,"[38] and that a person's sex is an unchanging gift given by God. Therefore, human beings should not attempt to change their gender. Rost went on to explain that he had

> "[Aimee Stephens's intent to cross-dress at work] would impose a substantial burden on the ability of the Funeral Home to conduct business in accordance with its sincerely-held religious beliefs."[39]
>
> —US district judge Sean F. Cox

Sixteen US States Ask the Supreme Court to Drop Workplace Protections for LGBT People

The attorneys general of the sixteen states argued that the term *sex* in Title VII of the 1964 Civil Rights Act was not, as recent court decisions suggested, meant to protect lesbian, bisexual, gay, and transgender people. Rather, they said, *sex* in Title VII simply denoted a person's gender— meaning that both female and male workers should be protected.

Source: Emily Birnbaum, "States Ask Supreme Court to Limit LGBTQ Workplace Protections," *The Hill* (Washington, DC), August 28, 2018. https://thehill.com.

no choice but to fire Stephens because her behavior went against God's intentions for humans.

Stephens sued the company, claiming it had discriminated against her on the basis of her sex. But she lost the case. US district judge Sean F. Cox rightly ruled that, under the 1993 federal Religious Freedom Restoration Act, for-profit corporations may claim a legal right to fire employees for being transgender. Cox wrote that Rost had convincingly shown that Stephens's conduct "would impose a substantial burden on the ability of the Funeral Home to conduct business in accordance with its sincerely-held religious beliefs."[39]

The Matter of Special Rights

People who agree with Cox's ruling can take heart. Indeed, Rost's victory against Stephens has been followed by other examples of support for traditional Christian values so often challenged by members of the LGBT community. Some of those supportive cases have involved so-called special protections. In recent decades some gay, lesbian, and transgender people have attempted to gain special rights, including in the workplace, that are not afforded to most other people. But only a few minority groups, including African Americans and disabled people, have gained the status of a legally protected class. Such protection is reserved for people who have experienced discrimination based on a characteristic that is inherent to their being.

"Activists are attempting to hijack the civil rights train by claiming that homosexual behavior deserves . . . special protection."[40]

—Mathew D. Staver, the founder of Liberty Counsel

Clearly, regardless of what they may claim, members of the LGBT community do not constitute such a class. According to Mathew D. Staver, the founder of Liberty Counsel, a nonprofit organization dedicated to advancing religious freedom, "The federal Civil Rights Act of 1964 laid the foundation for future civil rights laws. [LGBT] activists are attempting to hijack the civil rights train by claiming that homosexual behavior deserves the same special protection granted to racial and gender minorities."[40]

Existing Laws Are Perfectly Adequate

Furthermore, LGBT people have little of substance to complain about because cases of clear-cut discrimination against them in the workplace are extremely rare. That is because a large number of cities, counties, and states across the country have passed laws under which members of the LGBT community can seek redress if they feel their rights have been violated. Massachusetts, for instance, has a state law that forbids discrimination on the basis of sexual orientation and gender identity in employment, housing, public accommodations, credit, and union practices. The existence of statutes like that one renders passing more comprehensive federal laws against LGBT discrimination unnecessary.

Indeed, the local laws in question address the problem of discrimination in a wide range of social areas, including housing and public accommodations, private schools, retail stores, health care offices, restaurants, homeless shelters, and day care centers, among others. If a gay, lesbian, or transgender person feels that he or she has been discriminated against on the job, hiring an attorney is an option. In most cases, that attorney will be able to find redress for the client's complaint under one of the many local or state laws.

Relying on existing local laws is preferable to passing new federal anti-discrimination laws. After all, adding more laws when perfectly adequate ones already exist only acts to bog down the justice system. A streamlined justice system will only help the wheels of justice move swifter for LGBT and non-LGBT folks alike.

The Real Danger

States and cities are not the only entities that have adopted workplace protections for LGBT individuals. Many companies have taken this step as well. Among the companies that have done so are Uber, Google, Ikea, Microsoft, IBM, PayPal, and Coca-Cola. And these are just a few of the companies that have acted to protect the rights of LGBT individuals in the workplace. Given the abundance of protections already in place, there really is no need at all for yet another layer of laws. The federal government does not need to heap more laws upon already existing laws and corporate policies. Enough has been done to protect this population— far more, in fact, than probably is needed.

The real danger lies not in too few protections but in so many that they begin to impinge on the rights of other groups. Giving so much special treatment to one group, in effect, has threatened the rights of other groups. In this case, people with strongly held religious beliefs are being demonized in the effort to add more and more protections for LGBT individuals. This situation must not be allowed to continue.

The idea of instituting worker protection laws for LGBT people is a nonstarter because such statutes are not needed and interfere with the rights of non-LGBT individuals. Employers who have religious beliefs that clash with LGBT issues, for example, must be allowed to exercise those beliefs. At the same time, LGBT employees are well protected by existing local and state laws; there is no need for special workplace protections.

Employment Protections Are Needed for LGBT Workers

"For as long as people have demanded freedom, dignity, and equality under the law, many arguments to deny these rights have been wrapped in a false flag of religious liberty."

—Wade Henderson, the president of the Leadership Conference Education Fund

Quoted in Leadership Conference on Civil & Human Rights, "New Report Connects Religious Exemptions from LGBT Equality to Historic Efforts to Deny Civil Rights," February 1, 2016. https://civilrights.org.

Consider these questions as you read:

1. Are there any circumstances in which an employer could act on the basis of religious views without violating workplace discrimination laws? Explain your answer.
2. Do you think it is fair that LGBT workers are protected in some states but not in others? Explain your answer.
3. Do you think LGBT workers want workplace protections that other workers do not have? Why or why not?

Editor's note: The discussion that follows presents common arguments made in support of this perspective, reinforced by facts, quotes, and examples taken from various sources.

In 2019 an LGBT worker in Texas could be fired from his or her job simply because he or she was LGBT. It did not matter that the employee was highly qualified for the job or routinely did good work. The same thing could happen in Louisiana, Mississippi, Florida, Nebraska, and several other states. This is a clear violation of long-standing principles of equality under the law as well as common human decency.

The only way to rectify this situation is to make sure that LGBT workers nationwide are protected from the whims of biased state legislators and employers.

Efforts to Stop LGBT Equality Are Not New

One of the chief arguments for firing or not hiring LGBT workers is so-called religious freedom. This is the idea that one can fire or choose not to hire an LGBT individual if being LGBT conflicts with one's religious beliefs. By most anyone's definition, this is discrimination. Such discrimination is—and should be—against the law. Where laws are not crystal clear on this topic, they need to be made clearer, and they need to be standardized all across the country.

The most common argument against strong workplace protections for LGBT individuals is that such protections would violate religious freedom. Rather, they are using (or, some would say, misusing) religion in order to advance a narrow and bigoted agenda. People for the American Way (PFAW), a progressive organization that promotes equality for all Americans, points out that these religious zealots have frequently "portrayed legal and political defeats as attacks on Christianity and religious freedom."[41]

Efforts to slow or stop the advance of LGBT equality in the workplace and elsewhere in society by claiming it infringes on religious liberty are nothing new. They occurred all through the second half of the twentieth century. One example of this is the Manhattan Declaration of 2009. The signers of this document—including more than 150 noted American religious leaders—vowed to steadfastly refuse to accept any sexual unions that they deemed immoral.

Hiding Behind Religion's Mask

One major outcome of such narrow-minded thinking is that it has given certain employers ammunition to use against employees whom they perceive as immoral. The 2016 firing of funeral home worker Aimee Stephens by her boss, Thomas Rost, is a case in point. Inspired by the

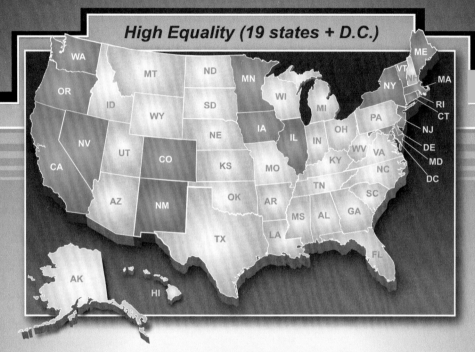

Too Many LGBT Workers in the United States Lack Legal Protections

Only nineteen states and the District of Columbia have significant laws protecting LGBT people, and only a few of those laws include workplace protections. Thus, only a federal law protecting all American workers, including those who are LGBT, can remedy this inequitable situation.

High Equality (19 states + D.C.)

Source: Transgender Law Center, "Mapping Transgender Equality in the United States," 2019. https://transgenderlawcenter.org.

Manhattan Declaration, Rost felt he was justified in terminating Stephens after she revealed that she was transgender.

The fact that Rost won the case emboldened others to take similar stands against LGBT employees who were simply being themselves. Efforts of this sort, a spokesperson for the PFAW explains,

> are being promoted by a network of national Religious Right organizations that oppose legal recognition for the rights of LGBT

people. . . . They work together to promote the false and destructive idea that legal equality for LGBT Americans is incompatible with religious freedom for those who oppose it, just as early civil rights opponents claimed that eliminating enforced racial segregation was an attack on southern white Christian religious beliefs.[42]

Do not be fooled by the slippery, deceptive rhetoric of these groups. They are squarely against granting equality to anyone with whom they disagree. They hide behind the mask of religious freedom in order to promote their homophobic agenda. Furthermore, they are perfectly willing to allow businesses and corporations to disobey any laws designed to protect employees who seek only to receive equal treatment under the law.

Treated like Everyone Else

One of the arguments frequently used to support the ability of employers to discriminate against LGBT workers is that such employees should not receive special rights or protections. Supposedly, they are rights not normally afforded to workers but which LGBT workers demand to receive. This is a completely baseless argument. According to Samuel A. Marcosson, a former law professor at the University of Missouri, "No law has ever been passed in any state that conferred on LGBT people a right that other groups of Americans did not enjoy."[43]

The ability to work at one's job without suffering various forms of discrimination and harassment is not a special privilege or protection. Equal treatment under the law is both a fundamental human right and a constitutional right. LGBT people have sometimes

> "[Various groups] promote the false and destructive idea that legal equality for LGBT Americans is incompatible with religious freedom for those who oppose it, just as early civil rights opponents claimed that eliminating enforced racial segregation was an attack on southern white Christian religious beliefs."[42]
>
> —People for the American Way, a progressive organization

demanded or lobbied to be treated equally and accorded the same civil rights and protections that non-LGBT people routinely receive. Those bosses who seek to discriminate against them invariably claim that these requests are for "special rights" that only gay, lesbian, and transgender people would enjoy. But this is a false equivalence. Marcosson notes that "if gay men and lesbians were granted the right to commit murder, that would be a 'special right' in the sense that it is not possessed by heterosexuals."[44] But, of course, LGBT people are not demanding such a right—or any other rights that their non-LGBT coworkers do not have.

> "People should not be ill-treated based on a characteristic or status they are unable to change."[45]
>
> —Samuel A. Marcosson, a former law professor at the University of Missouri

Further, it is important to remember that LGBT individuals do not choose to be or not be LGBT. Being gay, lesbian, or transgender is immutable; that is, LGBT people are born that way, just as African Americans are born with darker skin tones. Marcosson states that this is "the most compelling argument" against the notion that LGBT employees demand special rights. He adds that "people should not be ill-treated based on a characteristic or status they are unable to change."[45]

Local Laws Remain Inadequate

Nationally, legal protection for LGBT workers is spotty. Indeed, the Transgender Law Center reports, only nineteen states, along with the District of Columbia, currently have antidiscrimination laws protecting transgender workers. This means that in the other thirty-one states, employees can be fired simply for being LGBT, and those who are terminated have no legal recourse. They cannot even take advantage of the federal protections of Title VII of the Civil Rights Act, which prohibits employment discrimination based on race, color, religion, sex, and national origin. That is because Title VII does not specifically cover gender identity discrimination. Brian Hauss, an attorney for the American Civil Liberties Union, explains that "there is no federal law explicitly banning discrimination against transgender people" in the workplace. Therefore, Hauss says, "allowing employers to use religion to discriminate would put transgender people across the country—people like Aimee Stephens—at an even greater risk of losing their jobs just for being who they are."[46]

Even in states that have workplace protections for LGBT people, those protections are uneven and differ markedly from place to place. For example, eleven states offer employment protections that cover only public employees. There is no legal coverage for LGBT individuals who work at privately owned companies. Making matters worse, the laws in question in five of those states—Ohio, Virginia, Missouri, Alaska, and Arizona—address sexual orientation only. Trans workers who suffer workplace discrimination in those states are left out in the cold.

The patchwork of LGBT antidiscrimination laws no longer reflects American public opinion. A 2017 poll conducted by the nonprofit, non-partisan Public Religion Research Institute, located in Washington, DC, found that 70 percent of Americans back laws to protect LGBT people from discrimination in the workplace. A mere 26 percent of the respondents said they did not support such laws. It is therefore time for American lawmakers—in Washington, DC, and elsewhere—to pass antidiscrimination employment laws that *do* reflect the increasingly enlightened views of the American public.

Chapter Four

Should Businesses Be Allowed to Deny Services to LGBT People?

Businesses Should Be Allowed to Deny Services to LGBT People

- Exercising one's religious beliefs is not discrimination.
- Forcing a business to serve LGBT people violates the First Amendment right to freedom of religion.
- Actions based on religious beliefs should be exempt from discrimination laws.

The Debate at a Glance

Businesses Should Not Be Allowed to Deny Services to LGBT People

- Religious beliefs should not be an excuse to discriminate against LGBT people or anyone else.
- Refusing to serve an LGBT customer on religious grounds is a violation of that customer's constitutional rights.
- Actions based on religious beliefs should not be exempt from discrimination laws.

Businesses Should Be Allowed to Deny Services to LGBT People

"Tolerance and respect for good-faith differences of opinion are essential in a society like ours."

—Kristen Waggoner, a lawyer with the conservative-leaning Alliance Defending Freedom

Quoted in Adam Liptak, "In Narrow Decision, Supreme Court Sides with Baker Who Turned Away Gay Couple," *New York Times,* June 4, 2018. www.nytimes.com.

Consider these questions as you read:

1. Do you believe that refusing service to someone on the basis of sexual orientation is the same as refusing service to someone on the basis of race? Why or why not?
2. In what ways do the various freedoms guaranteed under the Constitution sometimes come into conflict?
3. Should religious beliefs be exempt from laws that prohibit discrimination? Why or why not?

Editor's note: The discussion that follows presents common arguments made in support of this perspective, reinforced by facts, quotes, and examples taken from various sources.

Denying services to someone out of hatred, spite, or simple meanness is not acceptable business practice. But when business owners with strongly held religious beliefs are asked to do something that violates those beliefs, this is not acceptable either. Religious freedom is a core value of American society. But somehow, over the past few years, business owners who attempt to live by their religious beliefs have been demonized for trying to hold fast to their faith. Their actions have been likened to Jim Crow–era bigots turning away black Americans—and worse. This is deeply hurtful and wrong.

Adhering to One's Faith

The LGBT community steadfastly refuses to even try to see things from the business owner's perspective. Business owners who have strong religious views are not out crusading against members of the LGBT community. And, for the most part, they are not even denying them all services. What some business owners have refused to do is provide special services that, in essence, condone behaviors that go against the teachings of their faith. In fact, in many of these situations, the business owners have tried to find a workaround that will satisfy both parties but without forcing anyone to compromise their religious views.

It is true that stores and other businesses exist in large part to cater to the needs of the local citizenry in what can be called the public square. But no one should expect the owners of those businesses to abandon the teachings of their faith in order to cater to customers

> "To say that men and women should not inject their 'personal morality' into public policy debates is a practical absurdity."[47]
>
> —Senator Barack Obama of Illinois

whose lifestyles are in direct opposition to those teachings. Even President Barack Obama, who was and remains friendly toward the LGBT community, agreed with this point. In 2006, then serving as a US senator, he stated,

[Nonreligious people] are wrong when they ask believers to leave their religion at the door before entering into the public square. Frederick Douglas, Abraham Lincoln, William Jennings Bryan, Dorothy Day, Martin Luther King—indeed, the majority of great reformers in American history—were not only motivated by faith, but repeatedly used religious language to argue for their cause. So to say that men and women should not inject their "personal morality" into public policy debates is a practical absurdity. Our law is by definition a codification [legal expression] of morality, much of it grounded in the Judeo-Christian tradition.[47]

Among the many leading American thinkers and patriots who agree with this view is Charles Haynes, the director of the Religious Freedom Center at the Newseum Institute in Washington, DC. Devout members of a religion, he says, are entitled—and even compelled—to cite the dictates of their conscience when faced with a moral dilemma. Like it or not, the decision to serve or not serve a person one sees as immoral is just such a dilemma. "We may not like the claim of conscience," Haynes says. "But you know, we don't judge claims of conscience on whether we like the content of the claim. We are trying to protect the right of people to do what they feel they must do according to their God. That is a very high value."[48]

A Basic Precept of Democracy

Forcing a business to serve LGBT people does more than infringe on the owner's personal beliefs. It also violates the First Amendment right to freedom of religion that appears in the US Constitution. The amendment grants each US citizen a right to follow the rules of the faith of his or her choice. Moreover, when the government tries to force someone to go against those rules, it tramples on that individual's constitutional rights.

The Supreme Court recently upheld and reaffirmed that basic precept of American democracy in what has become a classic case of failed LGBT legal overreach. It started with two gay men, Dave Mullins and Charlie Craig. In July 2012, while planning their wedding reception in Colorado, they went to a bakery near Denver to order a cake. The bakery's owner was willing to sell them a cake that had already been made, but he refused to make them a cake from scratch specifically for their wedding. He explained that doing so would violate his religious beliefs and rights as a US citizen.

The gay couple sued in an attempt to force the bakery to comply, and the Colorado courts ruled the owner had discriminated against the two customers. The case eventually went to the Supreme Court, which rightly ruled in favor of the bakery owner in 2018. Speaking for the majority of the justices, Anthony Kennedy wrote, "The laws and the Constitution can, and in some instances must, protect gay persons and gay couples in

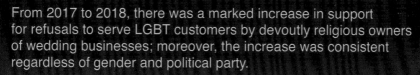

Rising Support for Refusing to Serve LGBT People

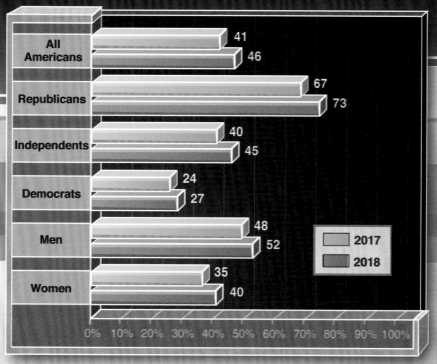

From 2017 to 2018, there was a marked increase in support for refusals to serve LGBT customers by devoutly religious owners of wedding businesses; moreover, the increase was consistent regardless of gender and political party.

	2017	2018
All Americans	41	46
Republicans	67	73
Independents	40	45
Democrats	24	27
Men	48	52
Women	35	40

0% 10% 20% 30% 40% 50% 60% 70% 80% 90% 100%

Source: Alex Vandermaas-Peeler et al., "Wedding Cakes, Same-Sex Marriage, and the Future of LGBT Rights in America," PRRI, August 2, 2018. www.prri.org.

the exercise of their civil rights. But religious and philosophical objections to gay marriage are protected views and in some instances protected forms of expression."[49] They are protected, he said, by the guarantee of religious freedom in the Constitution's First Amendment.

Many high-placed American legal figures agreed with the ruling. The US attorney general at the time, Jeff Sessions, pointed out, "The First

Amendment prohibits governments from discriminating against citizens on the basis of religious beliefs. The supreme court rightly concluded that the Colorado Civil Rights Commission failed to show tolerance and respect for [the bakery owner's] religious beliefs."[50]

The American Principles Project, a conservative think tank, also applauded the high court's decision. The group's executive director, Terry Schilling, stated, "Today's emphatic 7–2 ruling is a tremendous victory for [all] Americans who desire to follow their faith and conscience"[51] and to hold dear the freedoms granted in the Constitution.

One Person's Needs Versus Society's Needs

Even if people of religious faith and earnest personal conscience were *not* protected by the Constitution's guarantee of freedom of religion, they would certainly be worthy of such protection. People of religious conscience do not set out purposely to discriminate against anyone. Rather, they simply want their religious convictions to be respected. If that respect requires an exemption from existing laws, so be it.

In fact, allowing religious groups to be exempt from antidiscrimination laws is perfectly fair in a free society, Harvard University law professor Martha Minow argues. Such exemptions are justified, she says, "out of respect for the liberty of conscience" that lies at the heart of each member of a democracy. In formulating laws, the government should respect "the contributions religious organizations have brought to individuals and society over time." Organized religion has enlarged the common good, she goes on, so lawmakers "may find it wise to back off from direct governmental regulation of religious groups."[52]

Also, there is ample precedent for such exemption. In 2003, for example, New York State passed its Human Rights Law, which protects LGBT individuals from discrimination in employment, education, and housing. Yet the law includes an exemption for religious groups. These groups can deny employment to a gay or lesbian person if hiring him or her violates their religious principles. Religious groups can also choose not to rent or sell a house or apartment to an LGBT individual for the same reason.

Granted, such exemptions may seem unfair to those whose application to rent was turned down. But they must consider that their personal needs may sometimes be outweighed by the needs of the larger community. There are certain "basic goods" that lie at society's core, argue Heritage Foundation thinker Ryan T. Anderson and legal scholar Sherif Girgis. Devout religious conviction, they say, is one of those fundamental goods that help make human society flourish. Therefore, to prosecute a religious group for sexual discrimination may end up disrupting the "basic ingredients of human thriving."[53]

Both the person denied the rental and the LGBT community as a whole will likely be offended by such an exemption in the antidiscrimination law. Yet, as Anderson and Girgis point out, there is "no freestanding right not to be offended." Religious freedom for some, they argue, is often a challenging social and legal truth that others would rather not face. But that freedom must not be abridged simply to make one or two members of society comfortable. Religious liberty, Anderson and Girgis insist, "includes nothing if not the rights to worship [and] convert—forms of conduct (and speech) that can express the conviction that outsiders are wrong. Perhaps not just wrong, but deluded about matters of cosmic importance around which they have ordered their lives—even damnably wrong."[54]

> "[There is] no freestanding right not to be offended."[54]
>
> —Heritage Foundation thinker Ryan T. Anderson and legal scholar Sherif Girgis

Businesses Should Not Be Allowed to Deny Services to LGBT People

"This case has never been about the cake. It's about whether anyone in America can be turned away from a business because of who they are."

—James Esseks, the director of the American Civil Liberties Union's Lesbian Gay Bisexual Transgender and HIV Project

James Esseks, "President Trump and Attorney General Sessions Want to Enshrine a Business Right to Discriminate into the Constitution." *Speak Freely* (blog), American Civil Liberties Union, September 7, 2017. www.aclu.org.

Consider these questions as you read:

1. Can you think of any situations in which religious beliefs can legitimately be used as a reason for taking or not taking certain actions? Explain your answer.
2. In your opinion, is there a difference between refusing service to an African American or Jew versus an LGBT individual? Explain your answer.
3. Do you believe the US Supreme Court decided the wedding case correctly or incorrectly—and why?

Editor's note: The discussion that follows presents common arguments made in support of this perspective, reinforced by facts, quotes, and examples taken from various sources.

Many Americans have strong religious beliefs. Having those beliefs does not entitle them to discriminate against an entire group of people. And yet members of the LGBT community have been repeatedly subjected to discriminatory behavior by business owners who use their religion as grounds for such actions. This is wrong. Religious beliefs should never be employed as a reason to discriminate against LGBT people—or anyone else, for that matter.

Most Americans share this view, as noted in the 2018 report of the nonpartisan Public Religion Research Institute in Washington, DC, which found that 60 percent of Americans oppose permitting business owners to refuse services to LGBT customers even if such services would violate their religious beliefs. Stated another way: six in ten Americans oppose service refusals based on religion. On the other side, just one in three Americans (or 33 percent) support such actions. Jared Keller, a contributing editor at *Pacific Standard* magazine, comments on the rationale and morality of using religious teachings as an excuse for discrimination. "While the logic of 'religious freedom' may be legally sound," he writes, "this argument is widely regarded as morally bankrupt, legalistic camouflage for hatred and fear."[55]

> "LGBT equality [is seen by many Americans] as an inevitability."[56]
>
> —Jared Keller, a contributing editor at *Pacific Standard* magazine

Even most of those at the center of this controversy—that is, people who own small businesses—oppose religious-based service refusals. In October 2017 the widely respected Chesapeake Beach Consulting company conducted a poll on behalf of five hundred small business owners representing all regions of the country. When asked if a business owner should be able to deny goods or services to someone who is LGBT on the basis of the owner's religious beliefs, more than two-thirds of the interviewees answered no.

Finally, the percentage of people—business owners and customers alike—who desire to see all discrimination against LGBT people stop is growing. An increasing number of Americans see "LGBT equality as an inevitability," Keller points out. "It's clear that Americans can tell that arguments based on 'religious freedom' will not stop the country's ongoing march toward a more perfect union."[56]

More Discrimination Is Likely

Aside from the fact that it is morally wrong to use religion as an excuse to refuse service to a legitimate customer, such actions would also seem to defy the Constitution's guarantee of equal protection under the law.

Most Americans Oppose Religion-Based Refusals of Businesses to Serve LGBT Customers

According to a survey conducted by Morning Consult, a technology company that collects, organizes, and shares survey research data on issues in the news, a commanding majority of adult Americans oppose businesses refusing to serve LGBT customers on religious grounds.

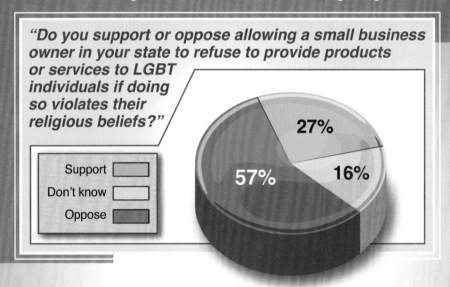

"Do you support or oppose allowing a small business owner in your state to refuse to provide products or services to LGBT individuals if doing so violates their religious beliefs?"

Support
Don't know
Oppose

27%
57%
16%

Source: Diana Piacenza, "Christians, White Evangelicals Have Contrasting Views on Issues in Cake Case," Morning Consult, June 4, 2018. https://morningconsult.com.

When given the opportunity to confirm this constitutional protection, however, the US Supreme Court ruled otherwise. This ruling involved a 2012 case in Colorado in which a gay couple asked a baker to make a cake for their wedding. The baker refused, citing his religious conviction that same-sex marriage is wrong. The couple sued, and in 2018 the case went to the Supreme Court, which ruled in favor of the baker.

This decision represents a grave error on the part of the Supreme Court. It is not the first time the high court has ruled incorrectly on an issue. After all, in 1857, in the infamous *Dred Scott* case, the court ruled that black people were not entitled to the same citizenship rights as white people. Similarly, in the 1944 *Korematsu* case, the Supreme Court said that putting Japanese Americans in prison camps during World War II was constitutional. The court later overturned these and other such wrongheaded rulings, admitting that they were serious miscarriages of justice. The 2018 decision involving the Colorado baker will, like the others, almost certainly end up being seen as a travesty and will be overturned.

That 2018 ruling was wrong because it allowed the concept of religious conviction to negate the right of equality under the law. Kristen Clarke of the Lawyers' Committee for Civil Rights Under the Law, a group that works to uphold constitutional protections, describes this ruling as a missed opportunity to send "a strong message discouraging and dissuading discrimination [against] people based on their LGBT status."[57]

The Supreme Court could have been—and should have been—a forceful voice against discrimination. Instead, its ruling is likely to lead to more instances of discrimination—and not just against members of the LGBT community. The potential damage to American fair play is "breathtaking in its scope and consequences," says James Esseks, a lawyer for the American Civil Liberties Union. "It would mean that a florist could refuse to sell flowers for the funeral of an interfaith couple, a dance studio could turn away the children of an interracial couple [and] a doctor could turn away transgender people altogether. And each and every law that makes discrimination illegal would be overridden by the constitutional right to discriminate."[58]

Esseks's point is well taken. Such a constitutional right to discriminate could drag the country even further into abridgements of cherished civil rights. It is conceivable that eventually businesses could refuse to follow food safety rules. Or any company could ignore consumer protection regulations, claiming that it is only following the religious beliefs of its owners. More than many other cases in history, the high court's wedding cake ruling has the potential to, in Esseks's words, "undermine America's core commitment to equality."[59]

Bogus Claims Rightly Rejected

The whole idea of religious beliefs being exempt from discrimination laws is wrongheaded. "When businesses open their doors to the public," Esseks writes, "they must open them to everyone on the same terms, regardless of race, color, national origin, disability, or under [laws protecting citizens'] sex, sexual orientation, or gender identity."[60] This is how equality works. This is what the Constitution guarantees.

To see that this is true, one only needs to look back at similar cases during the past several decades. Indeed, demands that business owners receive exemptions from civil rights laws are far from a new thing. Not that long ago, many businesses justified paying women less than men for the same work by citing the Bible. They quoted the biblical passage that says men are always the heads of households and that women should not work outside the home. Other businesses once refused to serve African Americans and Jews because the owners' religious beliefs supposedly forbade the social mixing of different races and religions. Over time, US courts correctly rejected these bogus religious-exemption claims. Recent attempts to seek such exemptions on the basis of one's attitude toward sexual orientation and gender identity are no different.

> "People should not face adverse treatment simply because of who they are."[61]
>
> —Ryan Thoreson, the lead researcher for Human Rights Watch

Moreover, just as exemptions from civil rights laws allowed businesses to pay women less, hurting both women and their families, refusing to serve LGBT people on the basis of such exemptions is hurtful. As Ryan Thoreson, the lead researcher for the humanitarian group Human Rights Watch, explains, "Anti-LGBT religious exemption laws are likely to exacerbate mistreatment because [they] undermine the core principle of nondiscrimination law: that people should not face adverse treatment simply because of who they are."[61]

This sort of inequitable and potentially harmful treatment of American citizens happens all the time, Thoreson points out. He cites a case in Michigan in which a lesbian couple brought their newborn baby to a pediatrician for the child's first checkup. When the doctor learned that the parents were of the same gender, she refused to see the six-day-old infant, claiming that to do so would go against her religious beliefs. Is this really the country we want—a country in which young babies suffer because those who could and should help them are allowed to mask their petty hatred of the parents under the guise of religious belief?

Source Notes

Overview: LGBT Issues

1. Tina Fetner, "Attitudes Toward Lesbian and Gay People Are Better than Ever," *Contexts,* vol. 15, no. 2, 2016. https://journals.sagepub.com.
2. Quoted in ProCon.org, "State-by-State History of Banning and Legalizing Gay Marriage, 1994–2015." https://gaymarriage.procon.org.
3. Fetner, "Attitudes Toward Lesbian and Gay People Are Better than Ever."
4. Fetner, "Attitudes Toward Lesbian and Gay People Are Better than Ever."
5. Quoted in Orthodox Christianity, "We're Tired of Gay Propaganda." http://orthochristian.com.
6. Gabriel Arana, "The Most Urgent Queer Political Battles to Fight in 2018," Them, January 1, 2018. www.them.us.
7. Dan Diamond, "Trump Administration Dismantles LGBT-Friendly Policies," Politico, February 19, 2018. www.politico.com.
8. Arana, "The Most Urgent Queer Political Battles to Fight in 2018."
9. Arana, "The Most Urgent Queer Political Battles to Fight in 2018."

Chapter One: Should Same-Sex Marriage Be Allowed?

10. Internet Encyclopedia of Philosophy, "Laws of Nature." www.iep.utm.edu.
11. Michael Jensen, "I Oppose Gay Marriage (and No, I'm Not a Bigot)," *Drum,* May 27, 2015. www.abc.net.au.
12. Jensen, "I Oppose Gay Marriage (and No, I'm Not a Bigot)."
13. Bertrand Russell, "Marriage and Morals," Portal Site for Russellian in Japan. https://russell-j.com.
14. Quoted in ProCon.org, "Should Gay Marriage Be Legal?" https://gaymarriage.procon.org.
15. Quoted in Sheryl G. Stolberg and Dalia Sussman, "Same-Sex Marriage Is Seen in Poll as an Issue for the States," *New York Times,* June 6, 2013. www.nytimes.com.
16. Kenneth T. Walsh, "Power to the States: Republican Presidential Candidates Are Leaning on States to Experiment on Issues Such as Gay Marriage and Marijuana," *Ken Walsh's Washington* (blog), *U.S. News & World Report,* April 10, 2015. www.usnews.com.
17. Eric Restuccia and Aaron Lindstrom, "Federalism and the Authority of the States to Define Marriage," *SCOTUSblog,* June 27, 2013. www.scotusblog.com.

18. Robert de Neufville, "Marriage Equality Is a Civil Right," Big Think, February 18, 2012. https://bigthink.com.
19. Neufville, "Marriage Equality Is a Civil Right."
20. Austin Cline, "Arguments Against Gay Marriage: Marriage Is for Procreation," ThoughtCo, February 7, 2019. www.thoughtco.com.
21. Quoted in Karen Kulm, "Pride Season and People of Faith," *Rolling Justice* (blog), CPC Justice & Witness Ministry. https://cpcjusticeandwitness.com.
22. JamieAnn Meyers, "Marriage: It's About Love and Commitment (a Transgender Perspective)," Huffington Post, February 2, 2016. www.huffingtonpost.com.
23. Meyers, "Marriage."

Chapter Two: Should Transgender People Be Allowed to Serve in the Military?

24. Quoted in Christianna Silva, "Trump Tweeted Transgender Military Ban After Just 10 Minutes Thought Following Briefing, Book Alleges," *Newsweek,* January 5, 2018. www.newsweek.com.
25. Quoted in Silva, "Trump Tweeted Transgender Military Ban After Just 10 Minutes Thought Following Briefing, Book Alleges."
26. Ralph Peters, "Obama's PC Military Rules Are Putting America at Grave Risk," *New York Post,* July 7, 2016. https://nypost.com.
27. Thomas Spoehr, "Should Transgender Americans Be Allowed in the Military? Not So Fast: Military Readiness Has to Be First Concern," Heritage Foundation, August 8, 2017. www.heritage.org.
28. Quoted in Liz Stark, "Hartzler: Transgender Service Members 'Costly' to Military," CNN, July 26, 2017. www.cnn.com.
29. Quoted in Stark, "Hartzler."
30. Spoehr, "Should Transgender Americans be Allowed in the Military?"
31. Brynn Tannehill, "The Supreme Court Just Ended My Military Career," *New York Times,* January 22, 2019. www.nytimes.com.
32. Jay Caputo, "Should Transgender Persons Serve?," *Proceedings,* December 2017. www.usni.org.
33. Caputo, "Should Transgender Persons Serve?"
34. Caputo, "Should Transgender Persons Serve?"
35. Martie Sirois, "Why We Need Trans People in the Military," Huffington Post, July 28, 2017. www.huffingtonpost.com.
36. Quoted in Mark Joseph Stern, "Federal Judge Blocks Trump's Trans Troops Ban, Calling It Inexplicable and Unjustified," Slate, October 30, 2017. https://slate.com.

37. Quoted in Stern, "Federal Judge Blocks Trump's Trans Troops Ban, Calling It Inexplicable and Unjustified."

Chapter Three: Are Employment Protections Needed for LGBT Workers?

38. Quoted in Mark Joseph Stern, "Federal Judge: Religious Liberty Includes a Right to Fire LGBTQ Employees," Slate, August 18, 2016. https://slate.com.
39. Quoted in Stern, "Federal Judge."
40. Quoted in ProCon.org, "Should Homosexuals Have 'Equal Protection' Rights Based on Their Sexual Orientation?" https://aclu.procon.org.
41. People for the American Way Foundation, "Who Is Weaponizing Religious Liberty?" www.pfaw.org.
42. People for the American Way Foundation, "Who Is Weaponizing Religious Liberty?"
43. Samuel A. Marcosson, "The Special Rights Canard in the Debate over Lesbian and Gay Civil Rights," *Notre Dame Journal of Law, Ethics & Public Policy,* 2012, vol. 9, no. 1, 2012. https://scholarship.law.nd.edu.
44. Marcosson, "The Special Rights Canard in the Debate over Lesbian and Gay Civil Rights."
45. Marcosson, "The Special Rights Canard in the Debate over Lesbian and Gay Civil Rights."
46. Quoted in Cristian Farias, "Religious Freedom Law Protects Business Owner Who Fired Trans Woman, Judge Rules," Huffington Post, August 20, 2016. www.huffingtonpost.com.

Chapter Four: Should Businesses Be Allowed to Deny Services to LGBT People?

47. Quoted in US Conference of Catholic Bishops, "Letter to President Obama, Senator Hatch, and Speaker Ryan," October 7, 2016. www.usccb.org.
48. Quoted in Tom Gjelten, "In Religious Freedom Debate, 2 American Values Clash," *Morning Edition,* February 28, 2017. www.npr.org.
49. Quoted in David Smith and Lucia Graves, "Supreme Court Sides with Baker Who Refused to Make Gay Wedding Cake," *Guardian* (Manchester, UK), June 4, 2018. www.theguardian.com.
50. Quoted in Smith and Graves, "Supreme Court Sides with Baker Who Refused to Make Gay Wedding Cake."

51. Quoted in Smith and Graves, "Supreme Court Sides with Baker Who Refused to Make Gay Wedding Cake."

52. Martha Minow, "Should Religious Groups Be Exempt from Civil Rights Laws?," *Boston College Law Review,* 2007, vol. 48, no. 4. www.bc.edu.

53. Quoted in Andrew Walker, "Respecting Religion," *Weekly Standard,* July 28, 2017. www.weeklystandard.com.

54. Quoted in Walker, "Respecting Religion."

55. Jared Keller, "'Religious Freedom' Is a Losing Argument Against LGBT Rights—Even Among Christians," *Pacific Standard,* June 12, 2015. https://psmag.com.

56. Keller, "'Religious Freedom' Is a Losing Argument Against LGBT Rights."

57. Quoted in Smith and Graves, "Supreme Court Sides with Baker Who Refused to Make Gay Wedding Cake."

58. James Esseks, "President Trump and Attorney General Sessions Want to Enshrine a Business Right to Discriminate into the Constitution," *Speak Freely* (blog), American Civil Liberties Union, September 7, 2017. www.aclu.org.

59. Esseks, "President Trump and Attorney General Sessions Want to Enshrine a Business Right to Discriminate into the Constitution."

60. James Esseks, "Can Businesses Turn LGBT People Away Because of Who They Are? That's Up to the Supreme Court Now," *Speak Freely* (blog), American Civil Liberties Union, June 26, 2017. www.aclu.org.

61. Ryan Thoreson, *"All We Want Is Equality": Religious Exemptions and Discrimination Against LGBT People in the United States,* Human Rights Watch, February 19, 2018. www.hrw.org.

Facts About LGBT Issues

LGBT History

- In July 1961 Illinois became the first state to decriminalize homosexuality.
- In 1972 Lambda Legal became the first legal organization founded specifically to fight for the equal rights of gays and lesbians.
- In December 1973 the American Psychiatric Association removed homosexuality from its list of mental disorders and ruled that being gay is a normal condition for a minority of the population.
- In March 1982 Wisconsin became the first state to outlaw discrimination based on sexual orientation.
- In May 2004 the first legal same-sex marriage in the United States took place in Massachusetts.

Same-Sex Marriage

- Fifteen countries currently allow same-sex couples to marry, including the United States, the Netherlands, South Africa, Canada, Belgium, Norway, Spain, Sweden, Portugal, Iceland, Argentina, Denmark, Uruguay, New Zealand, and France.
- By roughly two to one, more Americans support rather than oppose allowing gays and lesbians to marry legally.
- While just 35 percent of white evangelical Protestants favor same-sex marriage, this is more than double the level of a decade ago (14 percent in 2007) among this group.
- About one in ten LGBT Americans are married to a same-sex partner.
- About 84 percent of LGBT adults and 88 percent of the general public cite love as a very important reason for getting married.

LGBT Youth

- LGBT youth are twice as likely as their peers to say they have been physically assaulted.
- Four in ten LGBT youth say the community in which they live is not accepting of LGBT people.
- Roughly three-quarters of LGBT youth say they are more honest about themselves online than in the real world.
- Ninety percent of LGBT youth say they are open about their sexuality with their close friends, and 64 percent say they are open about it with their classmates.
- About 68 percent of LGBT youth say they hear negative messages about being LGBT from elected leaders.

Demographics

- About 0.6 percent of US adults identify as transgender.
- An estimated 1 million military veterans are lesbian or gay.
- The three US cities that have the greatest number of gay couples are New York City (47,000), Los Angeles (12,000), and Chicago (10,000).
- The major metropolitan cities with the highest LGBT concentrations are San Francisco (15.4 percent), Seattle (12.9 percent), and Atlanta (12.8 percent).
- Roughly 272,000 New York City residents are gay.

Related Organizations and Websites

Cato Institute
1000 Massachusetts Ave. NW
Washington, DC 20001-5403
website: www.cato.org

The Cato Institute is a public policy research organization dedicated to promoting individual liberty, free markets, and limited government. It conducts independent research on many policy issues, including those related to LGBT persons.

Eagle Forum
200 W. Third St., Suite 502
Alton, IL 62002
website: https://eagleforum.org

A conservative interest group that primarily focuses on social issues, including what it describes as pro-family, antifeminist values. The group publishes a variety of articles and other information promoting what it describes as traditional American values, including its opposition to many LGBT initiatives.

Family Research Council (FRC)
801 G St. NW
Washington, DC 20001
website: www.frc.org

The FRC is a Christian public policy ministry that works to defend religious liberty, the unborn, and families and their traditional values. The group publishes articles on a variety of social issues, including granting special rights to LGBT people.

The Heritage Foundation

214 Massachusetts Ave. NE

Washington, DC 20002-4999

website: www.heritage.org/

A conservative research and educational institution, or think tank, the Heritage Foundation promotes limited government and traditional American sexual and moral values. It holds that LGBT people should be treated with compassion but not granted any special legal or social protections.

Human Rights Campaign (HRC)

1640 Rhode Island Ave. NW

Washington, DC 20036-3278

website: www.hrc.org

The HRC provides a national voice on gay, lesbian, bisexual, and transgender issues. The group lobbies Congress and promotes community education projects relating to transgender people. Its website offers an illuminating section on the challenges faced by more than twelve thousand LGBT teenagers across the nation, whom the group surveyed in 2018.

National Center for Transgender Equality (NCTE)

1325 Massachusetts Ave. NW, Suite 700

Washington, DC 20005

website: http://transequality.org

The NCTE's members are dedicated to helping transgender people achieve social justice and equality, in part by educating members of Congress about transgender issues and needs. Its website contains sections providing detailed information on antiviolence measures, economic justice, and voting rights for young transgender people.

PFLAG

1828 L St. NW, Suite 660

Washington, DC 20036

website: http://community.pflag.org

Formerly known as Parents, Families, and Friends of Lesbians and Gays, PFLAG's mission is to promote the interests and well-being of LGBT Americans. The group's website features the latest news about battles for LGBT rights.

Transgender Law Center
1629 Telegraph Ave., Suite 400
Oakland, CA 94612
website: http://transgenderlawcenter.org

The center works to alter laws and people's attitudes relating to transgender people. The website provides information about the struggles of immigrants who are LGBT; how to volunteer to help transgender people in need; and how transgender people can find adequate, safe housing.

Transgender Legal Defense and Education Fund
20 W. Twentieth St., Suite 705
New York, NY 10011
website: www.transgenderlegal.org

This organization works to end discrimination based on gender identity and to bring about equality for transgender people in society. The website offers detailed information about the Name Change Project, in which attorneys in various states provide free services for transgender people who want to legally change their names.

For Further Research

Books

Michael Bronski, adapted by Richie Chevat, *A Queer History of the United States for Young People*. Boston: Beacon, 2019.

Cheryl B. Evans, *What Does God Think? Transgender People and the Bible*. Self-published, Amazon Digital Services, 2017.

Heidi C. Feldman, *LGBT Discrimination*. San Diego: ReferencePoint, 2019.

Gillian Frank et al., eds., *Devotions and Desires: Histories of Sexuality and Religion in the Twentieth-Century United States*. Chapel Hill: University of North Carolina Press, 2018.

Skylar Kergil, *Before I Had the Words: On Being a Transgender Young Adult*. New York: Skyhorse, 2017.

Susan Kuklin, *Beyond Magenta: Transgender Teens Speak Out*. London: Walker, 2016.

Elijah C. Nealy, *Transgender Children and Youth*. New York: Norton, 2017.

Jason Porterfield, *Marriage Equality:* Obergefell v. Hodges. Berkeley Heights, NJ: Enslow, 2019.

Pat Rarus, *The LGBT Rights Movement*. San Diego: ReferencePoint, 2019.

Internet Sources

Anna Brown, "5 Key Findings About LGBT Americans," *Fact Tank* (blog), Pew Research Center, June 13, 2017. www.pewresearch.org.

Daniel Cox and Robert P. Jones, "Most Americans Oppose Restricting Rights for LGBT People," Public Religion Research Institute, September 14, 2017. www.prri.org.

Dan Diamond, "Trump Administration Dismantles LGBT-Friendly Policies," Politico, February 19, 2018. www.politico.com.

Family Research Council, "Ten Arguments from Social Science Against Same-Sex Marriage," 2019. www.frc.org.

GLAAD, "Transgender FAQ." www.glaad.org.

Human Rights Campaign, "Understanding the Transgender Community." www.hrc.org.

Emilie Kao, "How Religious Freedom Erodes, One Step at a Time," Heritage Foundation, August 7, 2018. www.heritage.org.

Lambda Legal, "The Laws That Protect You." www.lambdalegal.org.

Aamer Madhani, "Poll: Approval of Same-Sex Marriage in U.S. Reaches New High," *USA Today,* May 23, 2018. www.usatoday.com.

Claire Cain Miller, "The Search for the Best Estimate of the Transgender Population," *TheUpshot* (blog), *New York Times,* June 8, 2015. www.nytimes.com.

Robert de Neufville, "Marriage Equality Is a Civil Right," Big Think, February 18, 2012. https://bigthink.com.

Bertrand Russell, "Marriage and Morals," Portal Site for Russellian in Japan. https://russell-j.com.

Martie Sirois, "Why We Need Trans People in the Military," Huffington Post, July 27, 2017. www.huffingtonpost.com.

Index

About the Author

In addition to his numerous acclaimed volumes on ancient civilizations, historian Don Nardo has published several studies of modern scientific, medical, and sexuality-related discoveries and phenomena. Among them are *Teens and Birth Control*, *Teens and Gender Dysphoria*, *Eating Disorders*, *Breast Cancer*, *Vaccines*, *Polar Expeditions*, and *The Scientific Revolution*. Nardo, who also composes and arranges orchestral music, lives with his wife, Christine, in Massachusetts.